BONE OVATION

Caroline Hardaker was born in the North East in 1986, and has lived there ever since, mostly in Newcastle. By day she writes for a fair trade organisation, and by night she is a successful fibre art sculptor, popular with collectors around the world. She always carries a rucksack with her, in case she should be swept off on an adventure. She can be found on Twitter @carolinehwrites, and blogs about her writing on carolinehardakerwrites.com.

Bone Ovation

CAROLINE HARDAKER

VP

Valley Press

First published in 2017 by Valley Press
Woodend, The Crescent, Scarborough, YO11 2PW
www.valleypressuk.com

First edition, first printing (September 2017)

ISBN 978-1-908853-89-9
Cat. no. VP0106

A CIP record for this book is available from the British Library.

Cover illustration by Ben Hardaker.
Cover and text design by Jamie McGarry.
Edited by Char March.

Printed and bound in Great Britain by
Imprint Digital, Upton Pyne, Exeter.

To Ben,

for listening to countless half-born poems that you don't understand, and buoying me up when the words get stuck. These stories are for you.

Acknowledgements

Firstly, a thank you goes to Kate Garrett, for publishing my first ever little poem and for encouraging my love of folklore, myth, and history. Long may it continue!

A stonking great big thank you goes to Jamie McGarry, for publishing my first book of words and for believing that my ideas were worth sharing. Thanks also for the over-embellished gin and tonics.

A third thank you to Char March, for understanding my odd little mind and teaching me more about my writing and myself than I thought an editor could. You've been invaluable to all the boney poems in this collection.

Thanks to Three Drops Press (*Tailfins and Sealskins* anthology), *The Hungry Chimera*, *In Between Hangovers*, *Pankhearst*, *Lungs* and *Your One Phone Call* who published some of these poems for the first time.

And finally, thank you to everyone (you know who you are) for the mental shoves and for listening to poems that (with your encouragement) do eventually transform from confused mulch into little stories that matter.

Contents

W h i t e s p a c e
for eyes' respite.

Acclimatise.

Sink.

Late/Early

Shock

stop, stop now,
soft hum. Glow.

Husks of shapes, but slanted; all looking sidelong
for a face averted, travelling. I watch them,
all wrong.
Tongue on gums, chewing half-eaten thumps;
words, blubs – beating to be out,
the taste of vinegar, salt licks and

sudden leg cramp

a mouth full of day, unespecial day, sodden,
dripped on dark, a black, a blank sheet;
a hole, *a horse – on fire, banners lit,*
who is the lady that rides the horse, it is white

roll, pull

Gobs digest and regurgitate a mirror-day;
a casket, a woman, a wreath,
she sits in a room I know but have not visited.

Cold.

The walls are irises.

The Rains

Each raindrop contains a soul
I'm told, and sleet is nought
but the urgent need of the dead to meet
their loved ones once more in the mortal world.
To stroke their skin, to leave a living trace;
a tear drop – a thin, translucent meridian.

My grandmother never used an umbrella
and would tip back her head and eat the rain.
She said it made her feel alive again.

Your Bones and My Bones are Chicken Bones

Holding hands, a wishbone splits us from collar to cuff
and only the clucking between marks stars from seed.
Our eggs are born in our mouths, crowned around
with a wreath of tawny feathers we invent with speech,
and no expanse of crowing will whittle the chicken
into lark, or goose, or inky raven.
The chicken is a chicken – splaying gnarled toes and plucking
   skull,
and no new squawks will help that lie be sown.

But our bones are the same, I grant you,
our bones are the same. Composite of brittle chalk
and precious like the stalks of daisies in chains
holding together a form paused in the effort of flight.

The Girl Who Fell in Love With the Mountain

I kissed the southern face of a mountain;

his coat scrubbed coarse; smelt of bones
and the iron blood from ruined stone.
The earth moved with me, fell beneath my lips
and I was received into earnest mud;
an ancient epidermis of soft heathers, grass,
and gallant crags enclosing me as his hill-bairn.
I lay immersed, fingering vast feathers
tickling to tender licks, his form; my body-palm
and all the while I rested there
the sunlight streaked my hair with white.

Clansmen

'Bring me at my close to the Water Dogs',
                              my father would say.

'When I'm tired, waning, take me to play
with those who ward the cusp of this earth –
the *Asrais*. You know them, my Love? Like most,
I want to meet my end surrounded by friends;
my ancestors, my clansmen –
leading me low to the world's bed.
I trust they'll show me where to rest my head.'

So in his last days, skin yellow and soft,
body wasted from the fight with his own particles,
I brought him to the loch, at dusk,
the air dense with a salty musk, and speckled
with the dance of wind-swept haar and dappled wings
refracting the sun like fragments of glass.
We decanted some vintage scotch
at the lapping edge of the firth, and settled –
waiting for the shore to break,
for the leap of a fish or a tail, for the rise of his pack.

How to Be Alone

Flicking the needle up by its eye
fashions a tighter stitch
(you don't want loose threads),
so start at the ankles of oversized pants
and back-stitch sleeves from benign insides –
snapping off the cord at the wrist.
You'll need assistance to hem yourself in
so make pleasantries (you don't need
to mean it), then tuck down head;
passing red thread through rubbery lip
and all of your chins – *all of them.*

Leave one survival nostril open.
Weave spare threads through hair, Viking-style,
then seek a hand to loop what's left
around lashes. Plait them if preferred.
Gather love notes and stuff them
in all hearing holes, block all empty spaces
(you don't want ghosts getting in).

This is only a solution until you're
unearthed. Your choice of corner
will determine the depth of solitude plumbed.
Once recovered, you'll either be found
softened, dreaming foetal bean-like dreams,
or when unzipped
there'll just be empty clothes
and unbroken seams.

My Place

I heard that arthritis is the motion when the driest bones
grate each brittle chalk stick to powdered grit
(like to create a fire with stones or split wood).
The resulting bone smoke catches the throat
and you grow an ashy rattle, sounding old and wild.
As the rest of the flesh is not used so much, it's consumed
– rather thin grub for impatient worms –
the last of those flicking slubbed veterans,
less substance left than paper. I can't blame them.
They've been watching the wasting too long to wait their turn.

My nurse disagrees with me, vehemently,
but what does she know?
Her knees are fine, and besides –
she's eighty years away from my corner of space and time.
Mine's the back place, there, with the plastic chair
'wipe it clean' and arms wide with an expectant absence,
white-wash negative walls, stainless steel rails,
the table laid out with aspirin, grubby copper cufflinks,
and unwanted spare change.

The Weight on My Feet

My tired feet
have shed skins inside my shoes
and now shy; *tired feet,*
tired, fire-feet.
They crack; a knapsack of bones.
They're stumps, stollen lumps
I press nightly to knead the butter out.

But they curl under, still,
coiling into paw-pads;
ripe plums to stand on.
Oh my feet, my tired feet
they hope to float so I soak them,
root them like bulbs
amongst nimbler water lilies
to let the rest of me talk.
My tired, tired, fire feet.
I have so much more to say.

The Paper Woman

Who is she, sir?

She tilts on her rocker, a brittle wooden frame –
hair all thinning, like fibreglass, tipping back and forward
shifting the dust
and once an hour dropping crepe lids
over ochre corneas, crusted, dry,
more to shut off the world than moisten eyes.

And no-one's to touch her?

She's always said so – even when supple
she brushed away stray fingers like matches
ablaze with danger. Only once did she stutter –
but stopped by God she ran, chin aloft
and quivering, lace skin shimmering.
All restraint gone to waste – smudged
by a Coalman's dark. The event is etched on her skin
with a sharpened stave, leaving bitter rivets which
itch to a depth she can't scratch.

And now she's cold, centuries old
(though in truth, fewer in years)
and any slight is a mortal wound. She was told
to wear her story like links in chainmail or bold tattoos
like the Bayeux Tapestry, but her skin got too thin,
it let the lead in, and the clumps glitter in the blood
like little blackened geodes.

And is there respite in sight?

Who's to know?
Perhaps there's a friend to erase those hurts
with salted bread, a warm, soft cloth – melting slack
the paper to expose her raw insides, the fragrant lush within;
the child who danced the Coalman's dance,
if there's still time. She's waiting for the One who'll try.

Womb-light

See the silver-licked black there, with the floating heads?
Come with me for a midnight dip with a collagen hit,

it's that cold. Slip into your sealskin, it's so thin and shows
the curves from the extra joys you treat yourself to.

The bulb of your hip joint cutting through water.
Your toes twisting sands like a pestle and mortar.

Aim for the moon, see it lash the surf? I'll race you to that spot.
Don't be dazzled by the glittering flickers either side

they're not stars but sucking weights that will drag you under.
Many others will have you as their plunder.

So come, please, leave the weight of you at shore,
slip off those chiffon wings, they're false feathers

and won't help you fly. So don't try. Sink,
swoop with me to that glowing moon and

I'll kiss you there amongst reeds and kraken-feelers,
moving you to the lowest flow in gloom.

Transfigurations

She folds up
around them, asleep,

nano-universes inside.
Curling in chin, hands around
a cup of talcum, soft as silk.
Too soon they'll erupt –
splintering elbows, knees,
bolting from bone joints creaking for oil
and choking her within iron oxide clouds.

An anatomical explosion.
Her fledglings flee, skirting around
their world's epidermis.
She collapses into pieces, all arid,
a junkyard of rock and woe.

After some years
they've stretched,
found their own scope, tested toes,
flown –

and left lighter, fragmented,
the younger (now grown)
can finger the parts that
make up the whole, know them again,
work to piece back together her bones,
stitching skin with feather strokes,
mapping her constellations
with elegant trimmings, warm hands,
and the press of their lips.

Aparted

I left you to slumber
in the crypt
my oh –
my dandelion oh,
with fat skulls, nightlights
and soft crackles
from shattered trashes underfoot,
as I step, all

pressed in the wet
phlats
of the earth.
Such soft mellow
caresses there were,
now I hold

grains, weighted peat, oh
smoked down
to dust and bone, oh
all days and dusks
all alone, oh.

Sticky White Rice

Rolling
little lumps that stick
in balls, onion-sized,
like eyes.
I squeeze, gently
between pads of fingers.
Soft, yielding,
tidy white

but

I want to crush it –
push it tight in my fist
humiliating it
into a spread of mess
smearing it in wild streaks
like Pictish paint.

But I won't.

It'll taste nice
with asparagus stalks
and prawns

so I'll put it down nicely,
and prepare the knives
and forks.

Balloon

Must you press upon my skin
your radicalisations? And under such duress?

Desist! End it quickly, gently lift your means.
If you persevere, I might cease to exist;

all your own scrawls spat back at your face
and I, a wrinkle, will shrink –
lynched from your fist.

Marriage & Black Holes

Remember my face, when you look up in bed
through the skylight, the net lace –
I'm the sucking goop between galaxies there,
spread thin like emollient blackcurrant jam
feeding seeds to our stellar satellites.
You could try to finger me,
I'm soft and flighted, wider than the night
and inset with the sparkling stars of life.
And yet you chose her, and strife,
and all the unknowns of a broken life,
a twister from our warren, that dense space
I've been compacting with memories just your size,
honeys, jams, and a wife the size of the sky.

Pestle and Mortar

Making it be herb by herb
and crafting laughter
sown from buds of wilted ends
(either for lovers or for friends),
no sparks or smokes
but a ring brown and thin
like vintage tin

firing

blanking up a part of brain –
then abruptly forgetting my own name.
Blindly grinding down choices

rough

sure enough with full intent
of consequence, so even if
I'm just playing at plants,
there's no skill spent with ill intent.
In such raw thinking, instinct knows
the way from brain to pulsing vein
to a noseful of sulphur, cupped in a palm.
How to make songs real, how to gift luck –
the joys sought by all who live.

The Woman is Like the Picasso

You'll not know her, she looks to the side
all eyes
a spectrum of illicit shades
hair all quantum in sharp directions
but swooning around the face
a moon, in carven perfection,
radiating with flowering action
and reaction
a myriad of connections between
the dazzling colours she's made.

See that fierce pride under bashful eyes?

Even Picasso couldn't capture it.
He tried
through abstract and dreams
to channel by subconscious
a force too violent
a face too vibrant to lay down
and his mind filled with it
and fell
warped flat.
Her form so potent for creation
it was like painting the rain in clouds,
lightning waiting.

She is facing away, but she is looking.

The Man Who Was Made of Bees

Everyone knew George, a silent judge, unassertive
but smiling George. A bachelor. Tall as the shorter trees in
Circa Valley, stout too. Pure charisma. He bristled with it.

He also rattled like bones in a jar, up-close.

Whispers supposed that he might be an envoi,
his glow born of more saintly stuff.
His shape shimmered, as if he baked in intense heat,
like sizzling meat topped with flaxen hair –
soaring like buttery steam.

His stillness gave some folk the creeps. *If he had an edge,*
it'd be barbed, they said. *Look right at him – you see your end.*

He didn't tend to stare that much, he'd sit, unmoving,
eyes painted pitch, matt, not living. His gait lacked a reassuring
boot-slap, and would appear in places without invitation –
your home, your shed – and hazy, like a hallucination.

You know Marge? Marge. Marge said he stung her
in the florist's shop, just brushing by.
She was left flushed and hyperventilating.
It left a rash, and she swore he flinched, itching at his skin.

Have you noticed that he bristles with white noise
when you lean in deep? He smells like drying wood.
I know he'd make the sweetest honey – if he liked you.
His fingers would tickle, light as eyelashes or the fur of a cat –
coat on end, teeth bared. Oh, his lips shine.
I'd stick to them.

I heard from Marge that the bees are disappearing.
I haven't seen them recently but I'm sure I've heard them buzzing.

Of Little Broken Things

I. TO BE FREE AND WARM IS A PRIMITIVE THING

He knelt by the darkened hearth, bricks and stone
feeding his old bones with clots and cold

and reaching into night retrieved the bird
purpled with decay, eyes buttoned up with time

and wings frozen open as if gliding; freedom on
silken feathers carrying flesh, grey as clay

and oven dried, swollen as a bag of sand.
With a pick he broke off the wings and spread

them wide at each side of the stony recess
as a gift. The fire can burn now.

II. IN BEAUTY THERE IS GRACE AND DEATH

She wore the feathers as an upstart would
cockily and green, wanting ardently to be seen

and hungered for by Brahmin broods, who'd eat up
her warmth and skin and shining eyes

her painted face marked up with lies
and the twelve dead Goldfinches dressed in her hair.

Let them see, let them stare.

III. OF THE FOUNTAIN OF YOUTH

Sinking little knees into street slurry, the boy ignored
the blood blooming in the mud around the dove

still clean and the colour of wheat. The bird was broken,
its clockwork unwound, rust in folds. Butter hands pressed

this prize to a cottony breast, eyes chalking from brain to
ruined wing. He had never thought much of death

and chose its undoing with the simplicity of a yoyo
throw. He latticed them both with his coat and scarf

and wondered whether he'd set the bird free
today or tomorrow, or if by then he'd be older

and would let it lie like others had, just letting it be.

Bone Ovation

After the second round of applause roared on
for longer than her smile lasted, she gathered silence
with the miserable lowering of lashes.

The room a-hush

her singing fell from cracked lips in a

cascade

of

bones,

body parts, and beetles. It was a melancholic sound
driven by the

tin-taste of wastes,

straw-thin, arid, edged with
sepia breath and the cloak of glamour, sequined
with tiny airborne spores, weighty with a dense stench –
one of tiredness and nature consuming nature,
swallowing itself like a forest bog.
It lay on us in trashes, tainting us with salty fret and
melody-seeds embedding in ill-informed pores.

She was singing about war, I think, or loss,
or maybe it was a losing battle with drink;

it didn't seem to matter, at the time.

It ended up in death, I remember,
whatever the sound was.